Grayslake Area Public Library District
Grayslake, Illinois

1. A fine will be charged on each book which is not returned when it is due.

2. All injuries to books beyond reasonable wear and all losses shall be made good to the satisfaction of the Librarian.

3. Each borrower is held responsible for all books drawn on his card and for all fines accruing on the same.

Animal Facts
to Make You Smile!

by Grace Hansen

abdopublishing.com

Published by Abdo Kids, a division of ABDO, PO Box 398166, Minneapolis, Minnesota 55439.

Copyright © 2015 by Abdo Consulting Group, Inc. International copyrights reserved in all countries. No part of this book may be reproduced in any form without written permission from the publisher.

Printed in the United States of America, North Mankato, Minnesota.

102014

012015

Photo Credits: iStock, Shutterstock

Production Contributors: Teddy Borth, Jennie Forsberg, Grace Hansen

Design Contributors: Laura Rask, Dorothy Toth

Library of Congress Control Number: 2014943783

Cataloging-in-Publication Data

Hansen, Grace.

 Animal facts to make you smile! / Grace Hansen.

   p. cm. -- (Seeing is believing)

ISBN 978-1-62970-731-0

Includes index.

1. Animals--Miscellanea--Juvenile literature. 2. Curiosities and wonders--Juvenile literature.   I. Title.

590--dc23

                       2014943783

Table of Contents

Bath Time

A giraffe cleans its nose and
ears with its extra-long tongue!

Bad Breath

Some turtles can breathe through their butts!

6

7

Funny Names

A group of porcupines is called a "prickle." A group of giraffes is called a "tower."

9

Sweet Snooze

Otters hold hands while they sleep. This is so they do not float away from each other.

Little Laughs

Rats laugh when they are tickled!

Pasture Pals

Cows form close **bonds**.

A cow makes more milk

when it is with its best buddy.

Greet with a Kiss

Prairie dogs say hello
with kisses.

Forgetful Rodents

Gray squirrels bury **acorns**.

Sometimes, they forget

where they buried them.

The acorns become new trees.

Together Forever

Puffin pairs stay together for life. Their babies are called "pufflings."

More Facts

- Scientists have found that rats, especially young ones, laugh when tickled. It does not sound like human laughter though. Rat laughter sounds like little chirps.

- **Collective nouns** can be fun! A group of penguins is called a "waddle." A group of zebras is called a "dazzle."

- All dairy farmers agree that calm cows are happy cows. Happy cows make more milk. Being with their best cow friends makes them happy. Calming music has been **proven** to make them happy too.

Glossary

acorn – the nut of an oak tree.

bond – a friendship made based on shared feelings.

collective noun – a noun that stands for a group of persons or things.

proven – show the truth by use of evidence.

23

Index

abdokids.com

Use this code to log on to abdokids.com and access crafts, games, videos, and more!

Abdo Kids Code:
SAK7310